2018 SQA Past Papers with Answers

National 5
SPANISH

FREE
audio files to accompany this title can be accessed at
www.hoddereducation.co.uk/sqaaudiofiles
You will find the files listed by language and level.

2016, 2017 & 2018 Exams

HODDER GIBSON
AN HACHETTE UK COMPANY

This book contains the official SQA 2016, 2017 and 2018 Exams for National 5 Spanish, with associated SQA-approved answers modified from the official marking instructions that accompany the paper.

In addition the book contains study skills advice. This has been specially commissioned by Hodder Gibson, and has been written by experienced senior teachers and examiners in line with the current National 5 syllabus and assessment outlines. This is not SQA material but has been devised to provide further guidance for National 5 examinations.

Hodder Gibson is grateful to the copyright holders, as credited below, for permission to use their material. Every effort has been made to trace the copyright holders and to obtain their permission for the use of copyright material. Hodder Gibson will be happy to receive information allowing us to rectify any error or omission in future editions.

Hachette UK's policy is to use papers that are natural, renewable and recyclable products and made from wood grown in sustainable forests. The logging and manufacturing processes are expected to conform to the environmental regulations of the country of origin.

Orders: please contact Bookpoint Ltd, 130 Park Drive, Milton Park, Abingdon, Oxon OX14 4SE. Telephone: (44) 01235 827827. Fax: (44) 01235 400454. Lines are open 9.00–5.00, Monday to Saturday, with a 24-hour message answering service. Visit our website at www.hoddereducation.co.uk. Hodder Gibson can also be contacted directly at hoddergibson@hodder.co.uk

This collection first published in 2018 by
Hodder Gibson, an imprint of Hodder Education,
An Hachette UK Company
211 St Vincent Street
Glasgow G2 5QY

Typeset by Aptara, Inc.

Printed in the UK

A catalogue record for this title is available from the British Library

ISBN: 978-1-5104-5496-5

2 1

2019 2018

Introduction

National 5 Spanish

The course specifications for National 5 Spanish changed in 2017, and Units and Unit Assessments were removed. The only change to the exam papers, however, was the removal of "overall purpose" questions for Reading and Listening. The 2017 and 2018 Past Papers reflect this, and the 2016 paper remains an incredibly useful revision tool. The questions contained in this book provide excellent representative exam practice. Using them as part of your revision will help you to learn the vital skills and techniques needed for the exam, and will help you to identify any knowledge gaps you may have, prior to the exam season in May–June.

It is always a very good idea to refer to SQA's website for the most up-to-date course specification documents. These are available at https://www.sqa.org.uk/sqa/47415

The course

The National 5 Spanish course aims to enable you to develop the ability to read, listen, talk and write in Spanish, that is to understand and use Spanish, and to apply your knowledge and understanding of the language. The course offers the opportunity to develop detailed language skills in the real-life contexts of society, learning, employability, and culture.

How the course is graded

The course assessment will take the form of a performance, a writing assignment and a written exam.

- The performance will be a presentation and discussion with your teacher, which will be recorded and marked by your teacher. It is worth 25% of your final mark.
- The topic for the writing assignment will be agreed between you and your teacher. It will be carried out in class, under supervised conditions. It is worth 12.5% of your final mark.
- The written exam will take place in May and this book will help you practise for it.

The exams

Reading and Writing

Exam time: 1 h 30 min	Total marks: 50	Weighting in final grade: 37.5%

What you have to do

- Read three passages of just under 200 words each, and answer questions about them in English.
- Write 120–200 words in Spanish in the form of an email, applying for a job or work placement: there will be six bullet points for you to address.

Listening

Exam time: 25 min	Total marks: 20	Weighting in final grade: 25%

What you have to do

- Part 1: listen to a presentation in Spanish, and answer questions in English.
- Part 2: listen to a conversation in Spanish, and answer questions about it in English.

How to improve your mark!

Every year, examiners notice the same kind of mistakes being made, and they also regularly come across some excellent work. They give advice in the three key areas of reading, listening and writing to help students do better. Here are some key points from their advice.

Reading

Make sure that your Reading answers include detail. Remember, an answer of only one word will not normally be enough to gain a mark. However, you do not have to answer in full sentences; bullet points are fine. Use each question as a guide to where to look, and what to look for. In the question there will be a clear guide to the context for the answer. Detailed answers are generally required, so pay particular attention to words like "más", "siempre", "bastante", etc. and to negatives. "Los sábados por la tarde" isn't just Saturday, and "a principios del mes de agosto" isn't just August, so be prepared to give all the details you can find.

Make sure you get the details of numbers, days, times etc. right.

Take care when using a dictionary when a word has more than one meaning. Learn to choose the correct meaning from a list of meanings in the dictionary.

Beware of false friends: "compartir" means share, not compare, and "esta de buen humor" does not mean he has a sense of humour, rather he is in a good mood.

In responding to the questions in the Reading papers, you should be guided by the number of points awarded for each question. You should give as much detail in your answer as you have understood, but you should not put down everything which is in the original text, as you would be wasting time. The question itself usually indicates the amount of information required by stating in bold, e.g. "State **two** things" or "Give **any two** reasons". If the question says "state any two things" it means there are more than two possibilities. Just choose the two you are happiest with and stick to them. Only give alternatives if you are absolutely unsure of what is correct.

If you have time at the end, you should re-read your answers to make sure that they make sense and that your English expression is as good as it can be.

Listening

This is the paper that improves most with practice. So use the Listening papers in this book several times to get used to the format of the exam.

Not giving enough detail is still a major reason for candidates losing marks. Many answers are correct as far as they go, but are not sufficiently detailed to score marks. The rules for Reading also apply here.

You hear each of the Listening texts three times, so make use of the third listening to check the accuracy and specific details of your answers.

Be sure you are able to give accurate answers through confident knowledge of numbers, common adjectives, weather expressions, prepositions and question words, so that some of the "easier" points of information are not lost through lack of sufficiently accurate details.

In responding to the questions in the Listening papers, you should be guided by the number of points awarded for each question, and by the wording of the question. You should give as much detail in your answer as you have understood, but you should not write down everything you hear. The question itself usually indicates the amount of information required by stating in bold, e.g. "**State two of them**".

Make sure you put a line through any notes you have made.

Writing

This, along with Talking, is often where students do best. It is a chance for you to know what your answers to the first four bullet points are in advance. Make sure you have some good material prepared and learned, ready to use in the exam. Also, where learners write pieces that are too lengthy, this certainly does not help their performance. So stick to 20–30 words per bullet point.

On the whole, the majority of candidates write well, and the range of language used is impressive. So look at the success criteria in the answer section and try to model your writing on it. This applies particularly to the last two bullet points. Practise writing answers to the final two bullet points, which are different in every exam, adapting material you already know rather than using a dictionary to translate ideas from English.

You should ensure that you are careful when you read the information regarding the job you are applying for, and make sure your answer is tailored to fit that.

Depending on the job, you may have to alter your strengths or the experience you are claiming. You should prepare in Spanish a description of some "soft" skills that are transferable, for instance, working with the public, able to communicate, good at working as part of a team or with others. Use your dictionary to make sure you know what the job actually is, if necessary.

Use the dictionary to check the accuracy of what you have written (spelling, accents, genders, etc.) but not to create new sentences, particularly when dealing with the last two bullet points. You should have everything you need prepared when you come into the exam.

Be aware of the extended criteria to be used in assessing performances in Writing, so that you know what is required in terms of content, accuracy, range and variety of language to achieve the "good" and "very good" categories. Ensure that your handwriting is legible (particularly when writing in Spanish) and distinguish clearly between rough notes and what you wish to be considered as final answers. Make sure you score out your notes!

You should bear the following points in mind:

- There are six bullet points to answer: the first four are always the same, the last two vary from year to year.
- Each of the first four bullet points should have between 25 and 30 words to address it properly.
- Answering the first four bullet points correctly will get you 12/20. Each of the last two, if answered correctly, will get an additional 4 marks.
- You should aim to write about 20 words for each of these last two points, but do not try to write too much, as this might mean you are more likely to get things wrong.
- You will be assessed on how well you have answered the points, and on the accuracy of your language.
- You should also try to have a variety of tenses in your preparation for the first four bullet points, including past, future and conditional if you can.
- For a mark of "good" or "very good", you should have some complex language, such as longer, varied sentences and conjunctions. So, have some sub-clauses ready, starting with words like "y", "o", "pero", "porque", "cuando", etc.

Good luck!

Remember that the rewards for passing National 5 Spanish are well worth it! Your pass will help you get the future you want for yourself. In the exam, be confident in your own ability. If you're not sure how to answer a question, trust your instincts and give it a go anyway – keep calm and don't panic! GOOD LUCK!

Study Skills – what you need to know to pass exams!

General exam revision: 20 top tips

When preparing for exams, it is easy to feel unsure of where to start or how to revise. This guide to general exam revision provides a good starting place, and, as these are very general tips, they can be applied to all your exams.

1. Start revising in good time.

Don't leave revision until the last minute – this will make you panic and it will be difficult to learn. Make a revision timetable that counts down the weeks to go.

2. Work to a study plan.

Set up sessions of work spread through the weeks ahead. Make sure each session has a focus and a clear purpose. What will you study, when and why? Be realistic about what you can achieve in each session, and don't be afraid to adjust your plans as needed.

3. Make sure you know exactly when your exams are.

Get your exam dates from the SQA website and use the timetable builder tool to create your own exam schedule. You will also get a personalised timetable from your school, but this might not be until close to the exam period.

4. Make sure that you know the topics that make up each course.

Studying is easier if material is in manageable chunks – why not use the SQA topic headings or create your own from your class notes? Ask your teacher for help on this if you are not sure.

5. Break the chunks up into even smaller bits.

The small chunks should be easier to cope with. Remember that they fit together to make larger ideas. Even the process of chunking down will help!

6. Ask yourself these key questions for each course:

- Are all topics compulsory or are there choices?
- Which topics seem to come up time and time again?
- Which topics are your strongest and which are your weakest?

Use your answers to these questions to work out how much time you will need to spend revising each topic.

7. Make sure you know what to expect in the exam.

The subject-specific introduction to this book will help with this. Make sure you can answer these questions:

- How is the paper structured?
- How much time is there for each part of the exam?
- What types of question are involved? These will vary depending on the subject so read the subject-specific section carefully.

8. Past papers are a vital revision tool!

Use past papers to support your revision wherever possible. This book contains the answers and mark schemes too – refer to these carefully when checking your work. Using the mark scheme is useful; even if you don't manage to get all the marks available first time when you first practise, it helps you identify how to extend and develop your answers to get more marks next time – and of course, in the real exam.

9. Use study methods that work well for you.

People study and learn in different ways. Reading and looking at diagrams suits some students. Others prefer to listen and hear material – what about reading out loud or getting a friend or family member to do this for you? You could also record and play back material.

10. There are three tried and tested ways to make material stick in your long-term memory:

- Practising – e.g. rehearsal, repeating
- Organising – e.g. making drawings, lists, diagrams, tables, memory aids
- Elaborating – e.g. incorporating the material into a story or an imagined journey

11. Learn actively.

Most people prefer to learn actively – for example, making notes, highlighting, redrawing and redrafting, making up memory aids, or writing past paper answers. A good way to stay engaged and inspired is to mix and match these methods – find the combination that best suits you. This is likely to vary depending on the topic or subject.

12. Be an expert.

Be sure to have a few areas in which you feel you are an expert. This often works because at least some of them will come up, which can boost confidence.

13. Try some visual methods.

Use symbols, diagrams, charts, flashcards, post-it notes etc. Don't forget – the brain takes in chunked images more easily than loads of text.

14. Remember – practice makes perfect.

Work on difficult areas again and again. Look and read – then test yourself. You cannot do this too much.

15. Try past papers against the clock.

Practise writing answers in a set time. This is a good habit from the start but is especially important when you get closer to exam time.

16. Collaborate with friends.

Test each other and talk about the material – this can really help. Two brains are better than one! It is amazing how talking about a problem can help you solve it.

17. Know your weaknesses.

Ask your teacher for help to identify what you don't know. Try to do this as early as possible. If you are having trouble, it is probably with a difficult topic, so your teacher will already be aware of this – most students will find it tough.

18. Have your materials organised and ready.

Know what is needed for each exam:

- Do you need a calculator or a ruler?
- Should you have pencils as well as pens?
- Will you need water or paper tissues?

19. Make full use of school resources.

Find out what support is on offer:

- Are there study classes available?
- When is the library open?
- When is the best time to ask for extra help?
- Can you borrow textbooks, study guides, past papers, etc.?
- Is school open for Easter revision?

20. Keep fit and healthy!

Try to stick to a routine as much as possible, including with sleep. If you are tired, sluggish or dehydrated, it is difficult to see how concentration is even possible. Combine study with relaxation, drink plenty of water, eat sensibly, and get fresh air and exercise – all these things will help more than you could imagine. Good luck!

NATIONAL 5

2016

N5

National
Qualifications
2016

Mark

X769/75/01

**Spanish
Reading**

THURSDAY, 26 MAY

1:00 PM – 2:30 PM

Fill in these boxes and read what is printed below.

Full name of centre

Town

Forename(s)

Surname

Number of seat

Date of birth

Day   Month   Year

Scottish candidate number

Total marks — 30

Attempt ALL questions.

Write your answers clearly, in **English**, in the spaces provided in this booklet.

You may use a Spanish dictionary.

Additional space for answers is provided at the end of this booklet. If you use this space you must clearly identify the question number you are attempting.

Use **blue** or **black** ink.

There is a separate question and answer booklet for Writing. You must complete your answer for Writing in the question and answer booklet for Writing.

Before leaving the examination room you must give both booklets to the Invigilator; if you do not, you may lose all the marks for this paper.

MARKS | DO NOT WRITE IN THIS MARGIN

Total marks — 30

Attempt ALL questions

Text 1

You read an article about a beach clean-up.

Cuarenta voluntarios para limpiar la playa

Unos cuarenta voluntarios trabajaron ayer para limpiar la playa de Sant Antoni en Ibiza. Los voluntarios al final de la jornada llenaron más de cincuenta bolsas con basura. El grupo, formado tanto por personas jóvenes como por familias, se reunió sobre las diez de la mañana en la playa.

Para algunos, como Carlos Aguado, era la primera vez que participaban. Carlos decidió participar en el voluntariado al ver el daño que ha sufrido la costa estos últimos años. Después de la limpieza, Carlos comentaba que "Lo que más he encontrado son colillas, vidrio roto y bolsas de supermercado".

La jornada de limpieza también contó con el apoyo de los turistas. Una pareja británica, tras enterarse de esta campaña, decidió ayudar: "Queremos proteger la belleza de la playa."

El objetivo de esta limpieza es concienciar a la gente sobre la importancia de no tirar los residuos al mar. "No esperábamos a tanta gente", explicó Eva Marqués, organizadora. "En mi opinión, creo que el medio ambiente interesa a mucha gente", añadió. Después de este éxito, es seguro que en el futuro Eva organizará jornadas de limpieza en los parques y visitas escolares para informar a los alumnos.

Questions

(a) (i) How much rubbish did the volunteers collect from the beach?   1

_____

_____

MARKS | DO NOT WRITE IN THIS MARGIN

Text 1 Questions (continued)

    (ii) At what time did the group meet?   **1**

_____

_____

(b) For Carlos Aguado, it was his first time cleaning up the beach.

    (i) What did Carlos see that made him decide to participate?   **1**

_____

_____

    (ii) What sort of rubbish does he say he found? Give details of any **two** things.   **2**

_____

_____

(c) Some tourists also took part in the clean-up. Why did a British couple decide to help? Give details.   **1**

_____

_____

(d) Complete the sentence.   **1**

The purpose of this beach clean-up is to make people aware of the

importance of not _____

_____.

(e) Eva Marqués organised the clean-up.

    (i) Why does Eva think that so many people turned up?   **1**

_____

_____

    (ii) What will she organise in the future? State **two** things.   **2**

_____

_____

Text 2

You read an article about International Girls' Day.

El Día Internacional de la Niña

De Visu/Shutterstock.com

Según una organización internacional, muchas niñas en varios paises del mundo hacen frente al problema de la falta de educación. Las Naciones Unidas han declarado el 11 de octubre como Día Internacional de la Niña.

El objetivo del Día Internacional de la Niña es de reconocer los derechos de las niñas, de intentar solucionar los problemas excepcionales que enfrentan las niñas, y de aumentar la proporción de niñas que completan la educación básica.

75 millones de niñas no van al colegio

Un estudio reciente demuestra que un tercio de niñas en el mundo no completa la educación secundaria y el 24 por ciento de las mujeres son analfabetas.

Muchas niñas se incorporan a la fuerza laboral a una edad temprana y suelen hacer los trabajos peor remunerados y menos valorados, por ejemplo en el servicio doméstico.

Un futuro optimista en El Salvador

Con el apoyo internacional, la vida de más de 5000 niñas de El Salvador ha mejorado muchísimo porque han podido estudiar un año más. Como resultado tienen la posibilidad de acceder a mejores empleos y de generar más ingresos para sus familias.

MARKS | DO NOT WRITE IN THIS MARGIN

Questions

(a) According to an international organisation, what problem do many girls face?

1

_____

_____

(b) What is the aim of International Girls' Day? State any **two** things.

2

_____

_____

(c) Complete the sentence.

2

According to a recent study, a third of girls in the world _____

_____

and 24% of women are _____ .

(d) Many girls join the work force at an early age. What types of jobs do girls often do? State any **two**.

2

_____

_____

(e) In what **three** ways have the lives of more than 5000 girls in El Salvador improved?

3

_____

_____

_____

[Turn over

Text 3

You read an article about the increase in people working from home.

Trabajar desde casa

Cada vez son más los empleados que "teletrabajan", o sea, que trabajan en casa. Este método de trabajar desde fuera de la oficina es aún más popular en España impulsado por mejor acceso a Internet y las tecnologías de la comunicación.

Además de reportar beneficios económicos, puede aumentar la productividad para las empresas. Y, para los trabajadores, trabajar a distancia permite que se pueda equilibrar la vida laboral con la vida familiar.

Elena Torres es técnico de recursos humanos. Lleva más de tres años teletrabajando para su compañía y está satisfecha con el sistema de teletrabajo. Dice: "Me conecto a Internet para estar comunicada constantemente con mis compañeros. Y puedo hacerlo desde casa o, entre cita y cita, desde un café o un parque."

De lunes a viernes, Elena sigue exactamente la misma rutina diaria: se levanta bastante temprano, toma su desayuno mientras lee su correo electrónico, se viste con ropa cómoda y anda un par de pasos hasta el salón de su casa.

"Gracias al teletrabajo, mi vida ha mejorado mucho. Me organizo el tiempo a mi manera", resume.

Questions

(a) Working at home is becoming more popular in Spain. What **two** reasons does the article give for this?

2

_____

_____

MARKS | DO NOT WRITE IN THIS MARGIN

Text 3 Questions (continued)

(b) The article describes the benefits of working from home.

    (i) As well as economic benefits, what is the other advantage for companies?

      1

_____

_____

    (ii) What is the main benefit for workers?

      1

_____

_____

(c) Elena Torres explains why she is satisfied with this way of working. What does she say? State any **two** things.

    2

_____

_____

_____

(d) She describes her daily routine from Monday to Friday. What does she say? State any **three** things.

    3

_____

_____

_____

(e) What does Elena think about working from home? Tick (✓) the correct statement.

    1

	Tick (✓)
Working from home has made her life more comfortable.	
Working from home can be difficult.	
Working from home has many advantages.	

[END OF QUESTION PAPER]

MARKS DO NOT WRITE IN THIS MARGIN

ADDITIONAL SPACE FOR ANSWERS

MARKS | DO NOT WRITE IN THIS MARGIN

ADDITIONAL SPACE FOR ANSWERS

[BLANK PAGE]

DO NOT WRITE ON THIS PAGE

N5

National
Qualifications
2016

Mark

X769/75/02

Spanish
Writing

THURSDAY, 26 MAY

1:00 PM – 2:30 PM

Fill in these boxes and read what is printed below.

Full name of centre

Town

Forename(s)

Surname

Number of seat

Date of birth

Day   Month   Year

Scottish candidate number

Total marks — 20

Write your answer clearly, in **Spanish**, in the space provided in this booklet.

You may use a Spanish dictionary.

Additional space for answers is provided at the end of this booklet.

Use **blue** or **black** ink.

There is a separate question and answer booklet for Reading. You must complete your answers for Reading in the question and answer booklet for Reading.

Before leaving the examination room you must give both booklets to the Invigilator; if you do not, you may lose all the marks for this paper.

Total marks — 20

You are preparing an application for the job advertised below and you write an e-mail in **Spanish** to the company.

Buscamos camarero/a

La heladería 'El Cucurucho', necesita **camarero/a** con conocimiento perfecto del inglés para este verano.

Las responsabilidades principales serán: preparar y servir los helados caseros en nuestro renombrado salón.

Se requiere una persona trabajadora con excelentes habilidades para la comunicación.

Envía tu currículum a *elcucurucho@heladería.es*

To help you to write your e-mail, you have been given the following checklist.

You must include **all** of these points:

- Personal details (name, age, where you live)
- School/college/education experience until now
- Skills/interests you have which make you right for the job
- Related work experience
- When you are available to work in the summer
- Your future career plans

Use all of the above to help you write the e-mail in **Spanish**. The e-mail should be approximately 120–150 words. You may use a Spanish dictionary.

MARKS | DO NOT WRITE IN THIS MARGIN

ANSWER SPACE

MARKS | DO NOT WRITE IN THIS MARGIN

ANSWER SPACE (continued)

ANSWER SPACE (continued)

MARKS | DO NOT WRITE IN THIS MARGIN

ANSWER SPACE (continued)

[END OF QUESTION PAPER]

MARKS DO NOT WRITE IN THIS MARGIN

ADDITIONAL SPACE FOR ANSWERS

MARKS | DO NOT WRITE IN THIS MARGIN

ADDITIONAL SPACE FOR ANSWERS

N5

National Qualifications 2016

Mark

X769/75/03

Spanish Listening

THURSDAY, 26 MAY

2:50 PM — 3:20 PM (approx)

Fill in these boxes and read what is printed below.

Full name of centre

Town

Forename(s)

Surname

Number of seat

Date of birth

Day	Month	Year		Scottish candidate number

Total marks — 20

Attempt ALL questions.

You will hear two items in Spanish. **Before you hear each item, you will have one minute to study the questions.** You will hear each item three times, with an interval of one minute between playings. You will then have time to answer the questions before hearing the next item.

You may NOT use a Spanish dictionary.

Write your answers clearly, in **English**, in the spaces provided in this booklet. Additional space for answers is provided at the end of this booklet. If you use this space you must clearly identify the question number you are attempting.

Use **blue** or **black** ink.

You are not allowed to leave the examination room until the end of the test.

Before leaving the examination room you must give this booklet to the Invigilator; if you do not, you may lose all the marks for this paper.

MARKS | DO NOT WRITE IN THIS MARGIN

Total marks — 20

Attempt ALL questions

Item 1

Gabriela talks about reading.

(a) Complete the table. — **2**

When does she read?	For how long?
	Half an hour
Every evening	

(b) When she was a child, who read poems and stories to her? — **1**

_____

(c) What does she now prefer to read? — **1**

_____

(d) Why does she not like science fiction novels? State any **one** thing. — **1**

_____

(e) Gabriela uses her tablet for reading. What else does she use it for? State **two** things. — **2**

_____

_____

(f) Which statement best describes Gabriela's reason for reading? Tick (✓) the correct statement. — **1**

	Tick (✓)
She reads to help her with her school work.	
She reads for enjoyment.	
She reads when she is bored.	

[Turn over for next question

DO NOT WRITE ON THIS PAGE

MARKS | DO NOT WRITE IN THIS MARGIN

Item 2

Ana tells Javi about the International Music Festival of Benicàssim.

(a) When did Ana first go to the Benicàssim Festival?

1

_____

(b) How long does the festival last?

1

_____

(c) What does Ana like most about the festival?

1

_____

_____

(d) Apart from the concerts, what else does the festival have to offer? State any **two** things.

2

_____

_____

(e) There is also a free camping zone at the festival. What can you do there? State **two** things.

2

_____

_____

(f) Ana talks about where she stayed the last time she went to the festival.

(i) Why did she not go camping?

1

_____

_____

(ii) Where did she stay? Give any **one** detail.

1

_____

_____

MARKS | DO NOT WRITE IN THIS MARGIN

Item 2 (continued)

(g) Why are her parents allowing her to go with her friends this year? Give any **two** reasons.

2

_____

_____

(h) What is Ana most looking forward to about the festival? Tick (✓) the correct statement.

1

	Tick (✓)
Staying in the campsite.	
Enjoying the atmosphere.	
Being away without her parents.	
Seeing her favourite band.	

[END OF QUESTION PAPER]

MARKS DO NOT WRITE IN THIS MARGIN

ADDITIONAL SPACE FOR ANSWERS

ADDITIONAL SPACE FOR ANSWERS

MARKS | DO NOT WRITE IN THIS MARGIN

ADDITIONAL SPACE FOR ANSWERS

[BLANK PAGE]

DO NOT WRITE ON THIS PAGE

National Qualifications 2016

X769/75/13

Spanish Listening Transcript

THURSDAY, 26 MAY

2:50 PM – 3:20 PM (approx)

This paper must not be seen by any candidate.

The material overleaf is provided for use in an emergency only (eg the recording or equipment proving faulty) or where permission has been given in advance by SQA for the material to be read to candidates with additional support needs. The material must be read exactly as printed.

Instructions to reader(s)

For each item, read the English **once**, then read the Spanish **three times**, with an interval of 1 minute between the three readings. On completion of the third reading, pause for the length of time indicated in brackets after the item, to allow the candidates to write their answers.

Where special arrangements have been agreed in advance to allow the reading of the material, those sections marked **(f)** should be read by a female speaker and those marked **(m)** by a male; those sections marked **(t)** should be read by the teacher.

(t) Item Number One

Gabriela talks about reading.

You now have one minute to study the questions for Item Number One.

(f) Suelo pasar mucho tiempo leyendo, tanto libro en papel como digital. Leo media hora por la mañana cuando me levanto y una hora y media cada tarde. Claro, los fines de semana puedo pasar todo el día leyendo, tumbada en el sofá con mi tablet. Cuando era niña, pasaba mucho tiempo con mi abuelo y él me leía poemas y cuentos infantiles. Ahora, leo de todo pero diría que mi tipo de novela preferida es la novela romántica. Sin embargo, a mí las novelas de ciencia-ficción no me gustan nada — las encuentro un poco aburridas y no son realistas. No entiendo a la gente que no lee nunca. Además de leer en mi tablet, descargo aplicaciones y a veces, compro por Internet. ¡No puedo imaginar la vida sin mi tablet!

(2 minutes)

(t) **Item Number Two**

Ana tells Javi about the International Music Festival of Benicàssim.

You now have one minute to study the questions for Item Number Two.

(m) Oye Ana, ¿tienes planes para el verano?

(f) Bueno, hace dos años fui con mi familia por primera vez al Festival Internacional de Benicàssim y he decidido volver este año.

(m) ¡Qué interesante! ¿Qué tipo de festival es?

(f) Um bueno, es un festival de música que dura cuatro días y ofrece música en directo.

(m) Ah, y ¿qué tipos de música hay?

(f) Hay de todo. Todo tipo de música.

(m) Y ¿qué es lo que más te gusta?

(f) Bueno, lo que más me gusta es que puedo ver artistas y grupos diferentes en el mismo día. Es fenomenal.

(m) Oye pues me gustaría ir. Me parece que no me aburriría nada.

(f) Claro que no. El festival no se limita a ofrecer conciertos. Además, hay cine, teatro, concursos, baile y exposiciones.

(m) Es verdad que hay algo para todo el mundo.

(f) Sí. Incluso hay una zona de acampada gratuita donde se puede descansar y conocer gente de todo el mundo.

(m) Suena estupendo. ¿Tú acampaste?

(f) La última vez, no. Fui con mis padres y no les gusta acampar. Por eso, nos alojamos en la casa de mi tío. Tiene una casa en el centro de un pueblo cercano.

(m) Y este año, ¿vas a ir otra vez con la familia?

(f) Um no. Con la familia, no. Me voy con un grupo de amigos. Mis padres dicen que ahora soy mayor y confían en mí. También soy más independiente. Por eso mis padres me van a dejar ir con mis amigos. ¡Qué bien!

(m) Será fenomenal.

(f) Seguro que sí. Lo que más espero es disfrutar del ambiente. Porque han anunciado unos grupos de maravilla.

(2 minutes)

(t) **End of test.**

Now look over your answers.

[END OF TRANSCRIPT]

Page three

[BLANK PAGE]

DO NOT WRITE ON THIS PAGE

NATIONAL 5

2017

N5

National Qualifications 2017

Mark

X769/75/01

Spanish Reading

WEDNESDAY, 3 MAY

1:00 PM – 2:30 PM

Fill in these boxes and read what is printed below.

Full name of centre

Town

Forename(s)

Surname

Number of seat

Date of birth

Day   Month   Year   Scottish candidate number

Total marks — 30

Attempt ALL questions.

Write your answers clearly, in **English**, in the spaces provided in this booklet.

You may use a Spanish dictionary.

Additional space for answers is provided at the end of this booklet. If you use this space you must clearly identify the question number you are attempting.

Use **blue** or **black** ink.

There is a separate question and answer booklet for Writing. You must complete your answer for Writing in the question and answer booklet for Writing.

Before leaving the examination room you must give both booklets to the Invigilator; if you do not, you may lose all the marks for this paper.

Total marks — 30

Attempt ALL questions

Text 1

You read an article about the use of mobile phones in the classroom.

Usar el móvil en clase

Ayer, en una conferencia educativa en Madrid, el experto educativo Juan Rodríguez Sanz describió el móvil como una herramienta muy poderosa en el aula. Hoy en día, existen más de 80.000 *apps* educativas para los móviles inteligentes que tienen muchas ventajas. Son gratuitas y ayudan a aumentar la motivación del alumno.

Muchos profesores insisten en la utilidad del móvil. En los últimos años, se ha creado el puesto de Coordinador Técnico en muchos colegios e institutos. Es un profesor que se encarga del desarrollo de la tecnología en las aulas y tiene que promover todos los usos diferentes de los móviles.

Sin embargo, hay algunos padres que se preocupan. Por ejemplo, Carlota Fuentes Girón cree que su hijo pasa demasiado tiempo con su móvil: "Ir al instituto es el momento ideal para hacer una pausa de la tecnología y relacionarse cara a cara con sus compañeros de clase."

Según el experto Juan Rodríguez Sanz, es lógico usar el móvil en las aulas porque todo el mundo lo usa en su vida cotidiana. Juan cree que en el futuro, la primera frase del profesor, al comienzo de la clase, será "encended los teléfonos móviles" en vez de "abrid los libros".

MARKS | DO NOT WRITE IN THIS MARGIN

Questions

(a) Complete the sentence.

Juan Rodríguez Sanz describes mobile phones as _____

_____ in the classroom.

1

(b) According to the article, what are the advantages of educational apps? State **two** things.

_____

_____

2

(c) Many schools now have an IT Coordinator. According to the article, what does this person do? Give **two** details.

_____

_____

2

(d) Carlota Fuentes Girón believes her son spends too much time on his phone in class. What does she think school is the ideal time for? Give details of **two** things.

_____

_____

2

(e) According to Juan Rodríguez Sanz, why is it logical to use mobiles in the classroom? Give details.

_____

1

(f) What does Juan believe a teacher will say at the start of a class in the future? State **two** things.

_____

_____

2

[Turn over

Text 2

You read an article about an online recruitment agency.

Un sitio web de empleo

PrimerPaso es un sitio web de empleo dirigido a estudiantes de dieciséis a veinticinco años. El objetivo de este sitio web es ayudar a los jóvenes a encontrar puestos de trabajo.

Encontrar un trabajo puede ser una tarea difícil porque muchas ofertas de trabajo requieren una licenciatura universitaria y varios años de experiencia laboral. En su sitio web se pueden encontrar ofertas de muchas empresas que buscan a jóvenes para puestos de trabajo a media jornada y de contratos de plazo fijo.

Juan encontró su primer trabajo a través del sitio web *PrimerPaso*. Nos cuenta: "Estaba deseando un trabajo simplemente para costear mi vida diaria. Publiqué mi CV en la web y el día siguiente me enviaron una selección de ofertas de empleo que coincidieron con mi perfil. Estoy contento porque encontré un trabajo que puedo compaginar con mis estudios."

PrimerPaso tiene una sección dedicada a consejos para prepararse para una entrevista. Es crucial enterarse sobre los valores de la empresa y hay que saber exactamente de qué trata el trabajo. Y el sitio web te avisa que no te preocupes si no consigues el puesto dado que encontrarás el trabajo de tus sueños algún día.

MARKS | DO NOT WRITE IN THIS MARGIN

Questions

(a) What age group is *PrimerPaso* aimed at?   1

_____

(b) What do many jobs require? State **two** things.   2

_____

_____

(c) On the *PrimerPaso* website, you can find job offers from many companies. What do these companies look for? State **two** things.   2

_____

_____

(d) Juan found his first job through the *PrimerPaso* website.

   (i) Why did he want a job?   1

   _____

   (ii) What happened when he published his CV online?   1

   _____

(e) The website also offers advice about preparing for an interview. Complete the sentence.   2

It is crucial to find out about _____ and

you have to know exactly _____ .

(f) Why should you not worry if you do not get the job? Give details.   1

_____

[Turn over

Text 3

You read an article about high street travel agencies.

Las nuevas agencias de viajes

Ya se sabe que las agencias de viajes, estas tiendas donde se puede reservar las vacaciones, han sufrido económicamente estos años. La crisis económica, la compra directa por Internet de billetes de avión, o la compra de noches de hotel desde el móvil han provocado una destrucción de las agencias de viajes.

Según un estudio recién publicado, el 66% de los viajes internacionales en el mundo ya se reservan desde Internet. Pero no todo está perdido para las agencias y el futuro parece un poco más positivo: existen nuevos negocios para el turismo de solteros o las visitas a balnearios.

Javier Mieres, propietario de *Endeavor*, una agencia especializada en organizar vacaciones fuera de lo normal, dice que "la gente se cansa de la playa y quiere algo que acorde con sus aficiones". Su agencia se creó hace seis años, en la crisis, y ha tenido un gran éxito. Javier pone como ejemplos que sus ingresos este año han aumentado y que va a abrir una sucursal nueva el mes que viene. Según Javier, hace falta que las agencias de viajes hagan lo siguiente para sobrevivir: ofrecer algo diferente y anticipar los deseos de los clientes.

MARKS | DO NOT WRITE IN THIS MARGIN

Questions

(a) According to the article, travel agencies have suffered losses in recent years. What reasons does the article give for this? State any **two**.

2

_____

_____

(b) The future seems more positive for travel agencies. What new business is there? State **two** things.

2

_____

_____

(c) Javier Mieres owns a travel agency.

    (i) What does his agency specialise in?

1

    _____

    (ii) What does he say about people's holiday habits? Complete the sentence.

2

    People are _____ and they want

    a holiday that _____ .

    (iii) Javier's travel agency has been very successful. What examples does he give of this? State any **one**.

1

    _____

    (iv) According to Javier, what do travel agencies have to do to survive? State **two** things.

2

    _____

    _____

[END OF QUESTION PAPER]

MARKS | DO NOT WRITE IN THIS MARGIN

ADDITIONAL SPACE FOR ANSWERS

MARKS DO NOT WRITE IN THIS MARGIN

ADDITIONAL SPACE FOR ANSWERS

Page nine

[BLANK PAGE]

DO NOT WRITE ON THIS PAGE

N5

National
Qualifications
2017

Mark

X769/75/02

Spanish Writing

WEDNESDAY, 3 MAY

1:00 PM – 2:30 PM

Fill in these boxes and read what is printed below.

Full name of centre

Town

Forename(s)

Surname

Number of seat

Date of birth

Day   Month   Year   Scottish candidate number

Total marks — 20

Write your answer clearly, in **Spanish**, in the space provided in this booklet.

You may use a Spanish dictionary.

Additional space for answers is provided at the end of this booklet.

Use **blue** or **black** ink.

There is a separate question and answer booklet for Reading. You must complete your answers for Reading in the question and answer booklet for Reading.

Before leaving the examination room you must give both booklets to the Invigilator; if you do not, you may lose all the marks for this paper.

Total marks — 20

You are preparing an application for the job advertised below and you write an e-mail in **Spanish** to the company.

Se requiere camarero/camarera

Buscamos camarero/camarera para trabajar en el *Hotel Girasol* en Ibiza durante los meses de julio y agosto.

Se necesita experiencia previa y hay que hablar español e inglés.

Los interesados deben mandar un email a girasol@hotelesespanoles.com

---

To help you to write your e-mail, you have been given the following checklist.

You must include **all** of these points:

- Personal details (name, age, where you live)
- School/college/education experience until now
- Skills/interests you have which make you right for the job
- Related work experience
- Your level of Spanish
- Why you want this job

Use all of the above to help you write the e-mail in **Spanish**. The e-mail should be approximately 120—150 words. You may use a Spanish dictionary.

MARKS DO NOT WRITE IN THIS MARGIN

ANSWER SPACE

[Turn over

MARKS DO NOT WRITE IN THIS MARGIN

ANSWER SPACE (continued)

MARKS DO NOT WRITE IN THIS MARGIN

ANSWER SPACE (continued)

[Turn over

MARKS | DO NOT WRITE IN THIS MARGIN

ANSWER SPACE (continued)

[END OF QUESTION PAPER]

MARKS | DO NOT WRITE IN THIS MARGIN

ADDITIONAL SPACE FOR ANSWERS

MARKS | DO NOT WRITE IN THIS MARGIN

ADDITIONAL SPACE FOR ANSWERS

Page eight

N5

National
Qualifications
2017

Mark

X769/75/03

**Spanish
Listening**

WEDNESDAY, 3 MAY

2:50 PM – 3:20 PM (approx)

Fill in these boxes and read what is printed below.

Full name of centre

Town

Forename(s)

Surname

Number of seat

Date of birth

Day	Month	Year	Scottish candidate number

Total marks — 20

Attempt ALL questions.

You will hear two items in Spanish. **Before you hear each item, you will have one minute to study the questions.** You will hear each item three times, with an interval of one minute between playings. You will then have time to answer the questions before hearing the next item.

You may NOT use a Spanish dictionary.

Write your answers clearly, in **English**, in the spaces provided in this booklet. Additional space for answers is provided at the end of this booklet. If you use this space you must clearly identify the question number you are attempting.

Use **blue** or **black** ink.

You are not allowed to leave the examination room until the end of the test.

Before leaving the examination room you must give this booklet to the Invigilator; if you do not, you may lose all the marks for this paper.

Total marks — 20

Attempt ALL questions

Item 1

Ana talks about technology.

(a) Where does Ana live? State any **one** thing.

1

_____

(b) Ana mentions the advantages of having a mobile phone. Complete the sentences.

2

Thanks to my mobile, I can _____ .

Also, it allows me to _____ on the

school bus in the morning.

(c) Ana's parents didn't allow her to have a mobile phone when she was younger. How did she spend her free time? State **two** things.

2

_____

_____

(d) When did she get a tablet computer? State any **one** thing.

1

_____

(e) Apart from technology, what other interests does she have? State **two** things.

2

_____

_____

MARKS | DO NOT WRITE IN THIS MARGIN

Item 2

Ana talks to Javi about television.

(a) How much time does Ana spend watching television per day? **1**

_____

(b) What does she say about the amount of television she watches? Tick (✓) the correct statement. **1**

	Tick (✓)
She does not think she watches too much television.	
She would like to be able to watch more television.	
She watches as much television as she can.	

(c) When does Ana watch television? State any **one** thing. **1**

_____

(d) Why does she never watch television before she goes to school in the morning? State any **two** things. **2**

_____

_____

(e) Why does she like music programmes? State any **one** thing. **1**

_____

(f)   (i) Why does she not like soap operas? State any **one** reason. **1**

_____

    (ii) What would she like to see more of? State any **one** thing. **1**

_____

_____

[Turn over for next question

MARKS | DO NOT WRITE IN THIS MARGIN

Item 2 (continued)

(g) Ana almost never watches television with her family.

(i) Why is this? Give **two** reasons.   2

_____

_____

(ii) What does she do instead with her family? State **two** things.   2

_____

_____

[END OF QUESTION PAPER]

MARKS | DO NOT WRITE IN THIS MARGIN

ADDITIONAL SPACE FOR ANSWERS

ADDITIONAL SPACE FOR ANSWERS

MARKS | DO NOT WRITE IN THIS MARGIN

National Qualifications 2017

X769/75/13

Spanish Listening Transcript

WEDNESDAY, 3 MAY

2:50 PM – 3:20 PM (approx)

This paper must not be seen by any candidate.

The material overleaf is provided for use in an emergency only (eg the recording or equipment proving faulty) or where permission has been given in advance by SQA for the material to be read to candidates with additional support needs. The material must be read exactly as printed.

Instructions to reader(s):

For each item, read the English **once**, then read the Spanish **three times**, with an interval of 1 minute between the three readings. On completion of the third reading, pause for the length of time indicated in brackets after the item, to allow the candidates to write their answers.

Where special arrangements have been agreed in advance to allow the reading of the material, those sections marked **(f)** should be read by a female speaker and those marked **(m)** by a male; those sections marked **(t)** should be read by the teacher.

(t) Item Number One

Ana talks about technology.

You now have one minute to study the questions for Item Number One.

(f) Yo uso bastante la tecnología y no hay duda de que tiene muchas ventajas para mí. Por ejemplo, vivo en un pueblo pequeño a unos treinta kilómetros de la ciudad. Entonces, gracias a mi móvil, puedo mantenerme en contacto con todos mis amigos. También, me permite escuchar música en el autobús escolar por la mañana.

Cuando era más joven, mis padres no me dejaban tener un móvil así que pasaba mi tiempo libre jugando en el jardín y cuando hacía mal tiempo, veía los dibujos animados.

Hace cinco años recibí una tablet como regalo de Navidad. A partir de ese momento, me interesé mucho más en la tecnología. Claro que es esencial que los jóvenes además tengan otros intereses. A mí me encanta leer revistas y tocar la guitarra en un grupo que he formado con unos amigos.

Pero, vamos, hay que reconocer que la tecnología tiene un papel muy importante en el mundo actual.

(2 minutes)

(t) Item Number Two

Ana talks to Javi about television.

You now have one minute to study the questions for Item Number Two.

(m) Bueno Ana, ¿te gusta mucho la tele?

(f) Sí, ¡me encanta la tele! En general, paso unas cuatro horas al día viéndola.

(m) Eso es mucho, ¿no?

(f) Pues, la verdad es que no me parece demasiado. Creo que es lo normal.

(m) ¿Cuándo ves la tele?

(f) Bueno . . . suelo ver la tele después de hacer mis deberes y a veces a la hora de cenar.

(m) Y tus padres, ¿qué dicen?

(f) ¡Mis padres piensan que soy adicta! Pero no es verdad. Por ejemplo, nunca veo la tele por la mañana antes de ir al instituto porque siempre me levanto tarde, tengo que hacer la cama y pasear al perro.

(m) ¿Y qué tipo de programas te gustan?

(f) Me interesan los programas de música porque son divertidos y me relajan.

(m) En cuanto a la tele, ¿hay cosas que no te gustan?

(f) Sí, no me gustan nada las telenovelas porque me parecen tontas y no son realistas. Por otra parte me interesaría ver más películas extranjeras y concursos de cocina.

(m) Y tú, Ana, ¿ves la tele con tu familia?

(f) No, casi nunca porque a mis padres y a mí, no nos gustan los mismos programas. Y mi hermano piensa que la tele es una pérdida de tiempo y prefiere salir con sus amigos.

(m) Entonces, ¿cómo pasas el tiempo con tu familia?

(f) Pues, comemos juntos y visitamos a la abuela cada fin de semana.

(2 minutes)

(t) End of test.

Now look over your answers.

[END OF TRANSCRIPT]

[BLANK PAGE]

DO NOT WRITE ON THIS PAGE

NATIONAL 5

2018

N5

National Qualifications 2018

Mark ☐

X869/75/01

Spanish Reading

MONDAY, 30 APRIL

1:00 PM – 2:30 PM

Fill in these boxes and read what is printed below.

Full name of centre

Town

Forename(s)

Surname

Number of seat

Date of birth

Day   Month   Year   Scottish candidate number

Total marks — 30

Attempt ALL questions.

Write your answers clearly, in **English**, in the spaces provided in this booklet.

You may use a Spanish dictionary.

Additional space for answers is provided at the end of this booklet. If you use this space you must clearly identify the question number you are attempting.

Use **blue** or **black** ink.

There is a separate question and answer booklet for Writing. You must complete your answer for Writing in the question and answer booklet for Writing.

Before leaving the examination room you must give both booklets to the Invigilator; if you do not, you may lose all the marks for this paper.

Total marks — 30

Attempt ALL questions

Text 1

You read an article about students and technology.

Técnicas de estudio

Cada vez más los estudiantes hacen uso de la tecnología para hacer frente a los exámenes. Sin embargo, los expertos educativos avisan de que es importante para los estudiantes poner límites al uso de la tecnología.

Es evidente que los estudiantes hoy día usan con frecuencia los ordenadores y las aplicaciones, ya sea para tomar apuntes o realizar mapas conceptuales en línea. Pero también estas tecnologías pueden distraer fácilmente y perjudicar la concentración. Según Anna Iñesta, directora de *Estudiantes para el futuro*, lo que más molesta a los estudiantes son los avisos de la entrada de nuevos correos electrónicos. Anna sugiere utilizar la aplicación, *Cortawrite*, que bloquea todo intercambio de informaciones y deja en paz al estudiante.

Para organizarse, existen muchas aplicaciones que son útiles. Francisco Gutiérrez, psicólogo estudiantil, recomienda que los estudiantes utilicen un calendario electrónico mensual. Aparte de poder organizarse, este calendario permite ver todos los días disponibles, manejar el horario y mejorar la calidad de trabajo. Aconseja también dedicar una mañana si es necesario a la elaboración del calendario. Francisco asegura que la ventaja principal de crear un calendario es que te sentirás mucho más tranquilo.

MARKS | DO NOT WRITE IN THIS MARGIN

Questions

(a) What do educational experts advise students to do?   1

_____

_____

(b) (i) According to the article, what do students frequently use computers and apps for? State **two** things.   2

_____

_____

(ii) According to Anna Iñesta, what most annoys students?   1

_____

_____

(iii) Anna suggests using the *Cortawrite* app to help. Complete the sentence.   2

The app blocks _____ and

leaves the student _____ .

(c) Francisco Gutiérrez recommends students use a monthly electronic calendar. Apart from being organised, what else does a calendar allow you to do?

(i) State **three** things.   3

_____

_____

_____

(ii) According to Francisco, what is the main advantage of creating this type of online calendar?   1

_____

_____

[Turn over

Text 2

You read an article about an open-air cinema on the beach.

El cine en la playa

Vinicius Tupinamba/Shutterstock.com

Este verano, la Playa del Gurugú en Valencia se convierte en una improvisada sala de cine al aire libre hasta el 28 de agosto. Cada día se puede ver una película diferente. Al anochecer, ponen unos centenares de sillas y hay películas proyectadas de manera gratuita. Es posible ver películas recién salidas y películas de los años setenta.

El chef, Juan Pozuelo, tiene un puesto en la playa y siempre vende mucha comida: "Estar al aire libre te da hambre y, en el cine, a todo el mundo le encanta picar." Juan ofrece una carta con palomitas caseras, batidos de sabores variados y refrescantes bebidas.

Y no es solamente un cine. Los fines de semana se puede disfrutar de una exposición sobre el vestuario utilizado en películas españolas famosas. Además, hay un mercado que vende joyería de plata y juguetes de madera.

Una amante del cine, Carmen Fuentes, resume su experiencia en el cine: "Me lo pasé genial. Lo que más me gustó fue el sonido relajante de las olas. ¡Qué maravilloso!"

MARKS | DO NOT WRITE IN THIS MARGIN

Questions

(a) (i) There is an open-air cinema on a beach in Valencia. What does the article say about this?

Tick (✓) the **two** correct statements.   **2**

	Tick (✓)
It opens on the 28th August.	
Every day you can see a different film.	
There are fifty chairs set out.	
The films are free.	

(ii) What kind of films is it possible to see there? State **two**.   **2**

_____

_____

(b) The chef, Juan Pozuelo, has a stall selling food on the beach.

(i) Juan says he always sells lots of food. What reasons does he give for this? State any **one**.   **1**

_____

(ii) What is on his menu? Give details of any **two** things.   **2**

_____

_____

(c) Apart from the cinema, there are other things on at the beach.

(i) What can you see in the exhibition? Give details.   **1**

_____

_____

(ii) There is also a market. What does it sell? Give details of any **one** thing.   **1**

_____

(d) Carmen Fuentes talks about her experience at the cinema on the beach. What did she like most about it? Give details.   **1**

_____

MARKS | DO NOT WRITE IN THIS MARGIN

Text 3

You read an information leaflet about an eco-club for young people.

Club Piensa Verde

Los problemas de nuestro planeta no son un fenómeno nuevo. Entre los temas más preocupantes de hoy día se encuentran la contaminación del aire y la destrucción de los bosques.

Para solucionar los problemas del medio ambiente, tenemos que cambiar nuestros hábitos, adoptar un estilo de vida más ecológico y hacer un esfuerzo colectivo. Por ejemplo, aconsejamos a la gente que solo compre lo necesario y que recicle lo más posible.

Aquí en nuestro club, tenemos una variedad de actividades educativas ambientales. Un ejemplo es el *Proyecto Contaminación* donde los jóvenes sacan fotos del daño medioambiental en su barrio, hacen un mural en el club e informan a sus familias de sus planes de limpieza en su entorno local. Estas actividades se realizan en pequeños grupos de trabajo.

Los miembros del club no solo aprendemos sobre el medio ambiente sino que desarrollamos actitudes positivas hacia nuestro papel en la sociedad. Esto contribuye a la formación de ciudadanos responsables. Así tenemos más conciencia de la importancia de proteger el planeta para las generaciones del futuro.

Questions

(a) The problems facing our planet are not new. Complete the sentence.   **2**

Among the most worrying issues nowadays are _____

_____ and _____ .

(b) (i) What do we need to do to find a solution to the problems of the environment? State any **two** things.   **2**

_____

_____

(ii) What does the leaflet advise people to do? State any **one** thing.   **1**

_____

MARKS | DO NOT WRITE IN THIS MARGIN

Text 3 questions (continued)

(c) The club has a variety of activities.

    (i) What do young people do in *Proyecto Contaminación*? State any **two** things.

        2

_____

_____

_____

    (ii) In what way do they carry out these activities?

        1

_____

(d) The club members learn about the environment.

    (i) What do they develop?

        1

_____

_____

    (ii) What do they become more aware of? Give details.

        1

_____

_____

[END OF QUESTION PAPER]

ADDITIONAL SPACE FOR ANSWERS

MARKS | DO NOT WRITE IN THIS MARGIN

MARKS DO NOT WRITE IN THIS MARGIN

ADDITIONAL SPACE FOR ANSWERS

[BLANK PAGE]

DO NOT WRITE ON THIS PAGE

[BLANK PAGE]

DO NOT WRITE ON THIS PAGE

[BLANK PAGE]

DO NOT WRITE ON THIS PAGE

N5

National
Qualifications
2018

Mark

X869/75/02

Spanish
Writing

MONDAY, 30 APRIL

1:00 PM — 2:30 PM

Fill in these boxes and read what is printed below.

Full name of centre

Town

Forename(s)

Surname

Number of seat

Date of birth
Day | Month | Year | Scottish candidate number

Total marks — 20

Write your answer clearly, in **Spanish**, in the space provided in this booklet.

You may use a Spanish dictionary.

Additional space for answers is provided at the end of this booklet.

Use **blue** or **black** ink.

There is a separate question and answer booklet for Reading. You must complete your answers for Reading in the question and answer booklet for Reading.

Before leaving the examination room you must give both booklets to the Invigilator; if you do not, you may lose all the marks for this paper.

MARKS DO NOT WRITE IN THIS MARGIN

Total marks — 20

You are preparing an application for the job advertised below and you write an e-mail in **Spanish** to the company.

Se requiere cajero/cajera

Se necesita cajero/cajera para trabajar media jornada durante el verano en nuestro cine, *Cine Estrella* en Sevilla.

Preferiblemente con experiencia previa y hay que llevar uniforme.

Se ruega mandar un correo electrónico a la dirección cine.sevilla@ salasdecineandaluces.es

---

To help you to write your e-mail, you have been given the following checklist.

You must include **all** of these points:

- Personal details (name, age, where you live)
- School/college/education experience until now
- Skills/interests you have which make you right for the job
- Related work experience
- The type of films you like
- What you do in your free time

Use all of the above to help you write the e-mail in **Spanish**. The e-mail should be approximately 120—150 words. You may use a Spanish dictionary.

MARKS | DO NOT WRITE IN THIS MARGIN

ANSWER SPACE

[Turn over

ANSWER SPACE (continued)

MARKS | DO NOT WRITE IN THIS MARGIN

ANSWER SPACE (continued)

[Turn over

MARKS | DO NOT WRITE IN THIS MARGIN

ANSWER SPACE (continued)

[END OF QUESTION PAPER]

ADDITIONAL SPACE FOR ANSWERS

MARKS | DO NOT WRITE IN THIS MARGIN

MARKS | DO NOT WRITE IN THIS MARGIN

ADDITIONAL SPACE FOR ANSWERS

N5

National
Qualifications
2018

Mark

X869/75/03

**Spanish
Listening**

MONDAY, 30 APRIL

2:50 PM – 3:20 PM (approx)

Fill in these boxes and read what is printed below.

Full name of centre

Town

Forename(s)

Surname

Number of seat

Date of birth

Day	Month	Year	Scottish candidate number

Total marks — 20

Attempt ALL questions.

You will hear two items in Spanish. **Before you hear each item, you will have one minute to study the questions.** You will hear each item three times, with an interval of one minute between playings. You will then have time to answer the questions before hearing the next item.

You may NOT use a Spanish dictionary.

Write your answers clearly, in **English**, in the spaces provided in this booklet. Additional space for answers is provided at the end of this booklet. If you use this space you must clearly identify the question number you are attempting.

Use **blue** or **black** ink.

You are not allowed to leave the examination room until the end of the test.

Before leaving the examination room you must give this booklet to the Invigilator; if you do not, you may lose all the marks for this paper.

MARKS | DO NOT WRITE IN THIS MARGIN

Total marks — 20

Attempt ALL questions

Item 1

Elena talks about her work experience.

(a) How long did Elena's work experience last?   **1**

_____

(b) Why did she have to get up early in the morning?   **1**

_____

(c) What tasks did she have to do? State **three** things.   **3**

_____

_____

_____

(d) Elena talks about her work colleagues.

   (i) What does she say about them? State any **one** thing.   **1**

_____

   (ii) What did she do with her work colleagues on her last day?   **1**

_____

(e) Complete the sentence.   **1**

Elena's classmates think work experience is a waste of time because they

_____ .

MARKS | DO NOT WRITE IN THIS MARGIN

Item 2

Paco talks to Elena about his part-time job and future plans.

(a) What does Paco say about his part-time job? State any **two** things.   **2**

_____

_____

(b) Paco describes his ideal job. What does he say about it? State any **two** things.   **2**

_____

_____

(c) Where would he like to work?   **1**

_____

(d) Paco wants to go to university.

   (i) What is he going to study? State **two** things.   **2**

_____

_____

   (ii) What do Paco's parents say about him going to university? State any **two** things.   **2**

_____

_____

(e) (i) What plan does Paco have for after university?   **1**

_____

   (ii) What is the problem with his plan? State **two** things.   **2**

_____

_____

[END OF QUESTION PAPER]

MARKS DO NOT WRITE IN THIS MARGIN

ADDITIONAL SPACE FOR ANSWERS

MARKS DO NOT WRITE IN THIS MARGIN

ADDITIONAL SPACE FOR ANSWERS

[BLANK PAGE]

DO NOT WRITE ON THIS PAGE

**National
Qualifications
2018**

X869/75/13

Spanish
Listening Transcript

MONDAY, 30 APRIL

2:50 PM — 3:20 PM (approx)

This paper must not be seen by any candidate.

The material overleaf is provided for use in an emergency only (eg the recording or equipment proving faulty) or where permission has been given in advance by SQA for the material to be read to candidates with additional support needs. The material must be read exactly as printed.

Instructions to reader(s):

For each item, read the English **once**, then read the Spanish **three times**, with an interval of 1 minute between the three readings. On completion of the third reading, pause for the length of time indicated in brackets after the item, to allow the candidates to write their answers.

Where special arrangements have been agreed in advance to allow the reading of the material, those sections marked **(f)** should be read by a female speaker and those marked **(m)** by a male; those sections marked **(t)** should be read by the teacher.

(t) Item number one

Elena talks about her work experience.

You now have one minute to study the questions for item number one.

(f) En mi instituto, tenemos que hacer prácticas laborales y el año pasado trabajé en una oficina durante diez días. Todos los días me levantaba temprano porque la oficina estaba muy lejos de mi casa.

Hacía muchas tareas diferentes, por ejemplo, tenía que contestar al teléfono, mandar correos electrónicos y a veces tenía que preparar café para todo el mundo. ¡Qué duro fue el trabajo!

Pero, a decir verdad, me lo pasé fenomenal porque todo el mundo era muy simpático y me llevaba muy bien con mis colegas allí. De hecho, el último día cenamos juntos en un restaurante.

Tengo compañeros de clase que piensan que las prácticas laborales son una pérdida de tiempo porque no ganan dinero. Pero yo aprendí mucho. Gracias a mis prácticas ahora, tengo experiencia en el mundo laboral.

(2 minutes)

(t) Item number two

Paco talks to Elena about his part-time job and future plans.

You now have one minute to study the questions for item number two.

(f) Oye, Paco, ¿tú tienes un trabajo a tiempo parcial?

(m) Sí, trabajo en una tienda de zapatos los fines de semana. Pienso que es fácil y variado. Sin embargo, no me gustaría hacer este tipo de trabajo en el futuro.

(f) ¿Ah, sí? Y entonces, ¿cómo sería tu trabajo ideal?

(m) Pues, en mi empleo ideal me gustaría trabajar en equipo. También, preferiría un trabajo con mucha responsabilidad y compañeros amables.

(f) Muy bien, y ¿dónde te gustaría trabajar?

(m) Tengo la intención de encontrar un trabajo en el extranjero porque me encanta conocer otras culturas.

(f) Piensas ir a la universidad, ¿verdad?

(m) Pues sí, voy a estudiar periodismo y política.

(f) Y ¿qué opinan tus padres de ello?

(m) Mis padres dicen que será una buena oportunidad. Tendré que independizarme y así conoceré mucha gente nueva.

(f) Y después de la universidad, ¿tienes un plan?

(m) Después de terminar mis estudios, quiero viajar por América Latina. Me hace mucha ilusión. Sin embargo, el problema es que necesitaría mucho dinero y tendría que ahorrar. Por eso estoy trabajando ahora.

(2 minutes)

(t) End of test.

Now look over your answers.

[END OF TRANSCRIPT]

[BLANK PAGE]

DO NOT WRITE ON THIS PAGE

NATIONAL 5

Answers

NATIONAL 5 SPANISH 2016

Reading

Question			Expected Answer(s)	Max Mark
1.	(a)	(i)	<u>over/more than</u> 50 bags/bin bags	1
		(ii)	(around) 10am/10 in the morning	1
	(b)	(i)	damage (to the coast)	1
		(ii)	• cigarette butts/ends • broken/smashed/pieces of glass • supermarket bags **(Any 2 from 3)**	2
	(c)		protect/maintain the beauty of the beach(es)/keep the beach beautiful	1
	(d)		throwing/dropping waste/rubbish into the sea/ocean/water	1
	(e)	(i)	the environment interests them/ they are interested in the environment	1
		(ii)	• park clean-ups/clear-up/tidy up the park **NB:** *ignore any mention of journey* • school visits/visits to school/going to school(s)	2
2.	(a)		lack/shortage of/don't get enough/ not having an education	1
	(b)		• to recognise the (human) rights of girls • to address/solve/find a solution to the problems faced by girls/ their problems • to increase the number/amount of girls who complete/get/have a (basic) education/schooling/ school **(Any 2 from 3)**	2
	(c)		• do not complete secondary/high school (education) • illiterate **NB:** *blanks must be in the correct order*	2

Question		Expected Answer(s)	Max Mark
2.	(d)	• the least/less well-paid/badly paid (jobs) • the least/less valued jobs/less value • domestic service/housekeeping/ household chores/housework/ house service/home service **(Any 2 from 3)**	2
	(e)	• study/go to school for 1 more year/a year longer/another year • a chance of/access to better jobs/employment/get better jobs • generate/earn/get <u>more</u> income/ money for their families	3
3.	(a)	• better/good/improved access to the Internet • communication technologies/ technology to communicate/ communicate through technology	2
	(b)	(i)	increases productivity/more productive/improves production **NB:** *ignore reference to employers/ employees*	1
		(ii)	balance work (life) with family/ personal (life)/work-life balance	1
	(c)	• she can be/stay in touch with/ communicate with/contact her colleagues/workmates/co-workers (online) • <u>she can stay in touch/work/do this</u> from home/café/park **NB:** *any 2 places needed*	2
	(d)	• she gets up/gets out of bed early • she eats/has breakfast • she reads/checks/looks at emails • she puts on/wears/picks comfortable clothes • she walks/goes to the living room/lounge **(Any 3 from 5)**	3
	(e)	**BOTTOM BOX** – Working from home has many advantages **NB:** *if more than one box is ticked, 0 marks are awarded*	1

Writing

Candidates will write a piece of extended writing in the modern language by addressing six bullet points. These bullet points will follow on from a job-related scenario. The bullet points will cover the four contexts of society, learning, employability and culture to allow candidates to use and adapt learned material. The first four bullet points will be the same each year and the last two will change to suit the scenario. Candidates need to address these "unpredictable bullet points" in detail to access the full range of marks.

Category	Mark	Content	Accuracy	Language resource — variety, range, structures
Very good	20	The job advert has been addressed in a full and balanced way. The candidate uses detailed language. The candidate addresses the advert completely and competently, **including information in response to both unpredictable bullet points.** A range of verbs/ verb forms, tenses and constructions is used. Overall this comes over as a competent, well thought-out and serious application for the job.	The candidate handles all aspects of grammar and spelling accurately, although the language may contain one or two minor errors. Where the candidate attempts to use language more appropriate to Higher, a slightly higher number of inaccuracies need not detract from the overall very good impression.	The candidate is comfortable with the first person of the verb and generally uses a different verb in each sentence. Some modal verbs and infinitives may be used. There is good use of adjectives, adverbs and prepositional phrases and, where appropriate, word order. There may be a range of tenses. The candidate uses co-ordinating conjunctions and/or subordinate clauses where appropriate. The language of the e-mail flows well.
Good	16	The job advert has been addressed competently. There is less evidence of detailed language. The candidate uses a reasonable range of verbs/verb forms. Overall, the candidate has produced a genuine, reasonably accurate attempt at applying for the specific job, **even though he/she may not address one of the unpredictable bullet points.**	The candidate handles a range of verbs fairly accurately. There are some errors in spelling, adjective endings and, where relevant, case endings. Use of accents is less secure, where appropriate. Where the candidate is attempting to use more complex vocabulary and structures, these may be less successful, although basic structures are used accurately. There may be one or two examples of inaccurate dictionary use, especially in the unpredictable bullet points.	There may be repetition of verbs. There may be examples of listing, in particular when referring to school/ college experience, without further amplification. There may be one or two examples of a co-ordinating conjunction, but most sentences are simple sentences. The candidate keeps to more basic vocabulary, particularly in response to either or both unpredictable bullet points.

Category	Mark	Content	Accuracy	Language resource — variety, range, structures
Satisfactory	12	The job advert has been addressed fairly competently. The candidate makes limited use of detailed language. The language is fairly repetitive and uses a limited range of verbs and fixed phrases, eg *I like, I go, I play*. The candidate copes fairly well with areas of personal details, education, skills, interests and work experience but does not deal fully with the two unpredictable bullet points **and indeed may not address either or both of the unpredictable bullet points.** On balance however the candidate has produced a satisfactory job application in the specific language.	The verbs are generally correct, but may be repetitive. There are quite a few errors in other parts of speech — gender of nouns, cases, singular/plural confusion, for instance. Prepositions may be missing, eg *I go the town*. Overall, there is more correct than incorrect.	The candidate copes with the first and third person of a few verbs, where appropriate. A limited range of verbs is used. Sentences are basic and mainly brief. There is minimal use of adjectives, probably mainly after *is* eg *Chemistry is interesting*. The candidate has a weak knowledge of plurals. There may be several spelling errors, eg reversal of vowel combinations.
Unsatisfactory	8	The job advert has been addressed in an uneven manner and/or with insufficient use of detailed language. The language is repetitive, eg *I like, I go, I play* may feature several times. There may be little difference between Satisfactory and Unsatisfactory. **Either or both of the unpredictable bullet points may not have been addressed.** There may be one sentence which is not intelligible to a sympathetic native speaker.	Ability to form tenses is inconsistent. There are errors in many other parts of speech — gender of nouns, cases, singular/plural confusion, for instance. Several errors are serious, perhaps showing mother tongue interference. The detail in the unpredictable bullet points may be very weak. Overall, there is more incorrect than correct.	The candidate copes mainly only with the personal language required in bullet points 1 and 2. The verbs "is" and "study" may also be used correctly. Sentences are basic. An English word may appear in the writing. There may be an example of serious dictionary misuse.

Category	Mark	Content	Accuracy	Language resource — variety, range, structures
Poor	4	The candidate has had considerable difficulty in addressing the job advert. There is little evidence of the use of detailed language. Three or four sentences may not be understood by a sympathetic native speaker. **Either or both of the unpredictable bullet points may not have been addressed.**	Many of the verbs are incorrect. There are many errors in other parts of speech — personal pronouns, gender of nouns, cases, singular/plural confusion, prepositions, for instance. The language is probably inaccurate throughout the writing.	The candidate cannot cope with more than one or two basic verbs. The candidate displays almost no knowledge of the present tense of verbs. Verbs used more than once may be written differently on each occasion. Sentences are very short. The candidate has a very limited vocabulary. Several English words may appear in the writing. There are examples of serious dictionary misuse.
Very poor	0	The candidate is unable to address the job advert. **The two unpredictable bullet points may not have been addressed.** Very little is intelligible to a sympathetic native speaker.	Virtually nothing is correct.	The candidate may only cope with the verbs *to have* and *to be*. Very few words are written correctly in the modern language. English words are used. There may be several examples of mother tongue interference. There may be several examples of serious dictionary misuse.

Listening

Question			Expected Answer(s)	Max Mark
1.	(a)		• in the morning/every morning/ when she gets up • an hour and a half/1 hour 30 mins	2
	(b)		grandfather/grandpa/papa/granda	1
	(c)		romance/romantic/love (novels/ stories/books)	1
	(d)		• a little/a bit/quite/slightly boring • not realistic/unrealistic **(Any 1 from 2)**	1
	(e)		• to download apps/applications • to shop/buy/shopping (online)/ buying things/stuff/internet shopping	2
	(f)		**BOX 2** – she reads for enjoyment *NB: if more than one box is ticked, 0 marks are awarded*	1
2.	(a)		two years/summers ago	1
	(b)		four days	1
	(c)		(she can see) different artists/ groups/bands/musicians/singers on the same day/throughout the day/ on the one day	1
	(d)		• cinema/films/movies • theatre/plays • competitions/contests • dance/dancing • exhibitions/shows **(Any 2 from 5)**	2
	(e)		• to have a rest/to relax/chill out • to meet/to get to know people from all over the world/from other countries	2
	(f)	(i)	her parents don't like it/camping	1
		(ii)	• in her uncle's house/home/with her uncle/at her uncle's • in a house in the centre of the town/village • in a house in a nearby town/ village **(Any 1 from 3)**	1
	(g)		• she is older/old enough/grown up • they trust her • she is more independent/ independent enough **(Any 2 from 3)**	2
	(h)		**BOX 2** – enjoying the atmosphere *NB: if more than one box is ticked, 0 marks are awarded*	1

NATIONAL 5 SPANISH 2017

Reading

Question			Expected Answer(s)	Max mark
1.	(a)		A <u>very</u> powerful tool	1
	(b)		• Free/cost nothing • Increase/improve pupil/student motivation	2
	(c)		• Development of/develops technology/IT/ICT • Promotes/shows/makes them aware of different uses of mobiles/phones	2
	(d)		• (Take/have) a break/a rest/time out/a pause from technology/IT/ ICT/put technology on hold • To relate/talk/connect to classmates/companions in class face to face	2
	(e)		Everyone uses them/it in everyday/ daily life	1
	(f)		• Turn/switch/put on the/your mobiles/phones • <u>Instead of/rather than</u> open the/ your books	2
2.	(a)		16–25	1
	(b)		• A (university) degree/university qualification/diploma • <u>Several/various/a few/some years</u> of work experience	2
	(c)		• (Young) people for part-time jobs/work/contracts/hours • (People for) fixed-term/period/ time contracts/people to hire/ who can work for a fixed time *NB: "people" need only be mentioned once in the candidate's answer*	2
	(d)	(i)	To fund/pay for/finance/cover his everyday/daily life/expenses	1
		(ii)	<u>A selection of/a lot of/many</u> jobs/ offers/job offers	1
	(e)		• The company's/firm's/business'/ enterprise's values • What the job/work is about/ involves/deals with	2
	(f)		You will/could/can find/get/have your dream job Some/one/any day	1

Question			Expected Answer(s)	Max mark
3.	(a)		• The economic/financial crisis/recession • Buying/booking/shopping for airline/plane tickets/flights <u>online/on the internet</u> • Buying nights in a hotel/booking hotels <u>from a mobile/phone</u> **(Any 2 from 3)**	2
	(b)		• Tourism for single people/singles/people on their own/bachelors/single men/single tourists • Spas/health/seaside resorts *NB: single tourists who visit spas/seaside resorts = 1 mark*	2
	(c)	(i)	Out/outside of the ordinary/norm/unusual <u>holidays/holidays</u> that aren't normal	1
		(ii)	• Tired/fed up/bored of the beach/seaside • Matches/in keeping/agrees/in harmony with their hobbies/interests/likes/likings	2
		(iii)	• It was created/opened during the (economic) crisis/recession • Income has increased/better income • (He is) opening/opens a new/another branch/shop/office **(Any 1 from 3)**	1
		(iv)	• Offer/do/have something different/different holidays/things/deals • Anticipate/foresee/predict customers'/clients' wishes/desires/wants	2

Writing

Please see the assessment criteria for Writing on pages 106–108.

Listening

Question			Expected Answer(s)	Max mark
1.	(a)		• Small town/village • 30 km from the city/town **(Any 1 from 2)**	1
	(b)		• Keep/stay in touch/maintain contact with friends • Listen to music	2
	(c)		• Played/playing in the garden • Watched/watching cartoons/animated films	2
	(d)		• Five years ago • Christmas **(Any 1 from 2)**	1
	(e)		• Reading magazines • Plays guitar **OR** • Is in a group/band with friends	2
2.	(a)		4 hours	1
	(b)		• She does not think she watches too much television *(Box 1)* **NB**: *if more than one box is ticked 0 marks are awarded*	1
	(c)		• After homework • At dinner/tea time **(Any 1 from 2)**	1
	(d)		• Gets up late • Has to make her bed • Has to walk dog (has to make her bed and walk the dog = 2 marks) **(Any 2 from 3)**	2
	(e)		• They are fun • They relax me/they are relaxing **(Any 1 from 2)**	1
	(f)	(i)	• They're stupid/silly • They're not realistic/unrealistic/not real **(Any 1 from 2)**	1
		(ii)	• Foreign films/foreign cinema/films from abroad/films from other countries • Cookery competitions/cookery game shows **(Any 1 from 2)**	1
	(g)	(i)	• Her parents don't like the same programmes/don't like what she watches • Her brother thinks it's a waste of time • Her brother prefers going out with friends **(Any 2 from 3)**	2
		(ii)	• Eat/have lunch/dinner • Visit gran/go and see gran	2

NATIONAL 5 SPANISH 2018

Reading

Question			Expected Response(s)	Max mark
1.	(a)		Set limits to using technology/limit the use/usage of technology/put limit(s) on the use of technology/ICT	1
	(b)	(i)	• Take (down)/make notes/note taking • Create/make/do/draw mind maps *NB: Make notes and mindmaps = 2 marks*	2
		(ii)	E-mail alerts/notifications/notices/pop-ups/popping up	1
		(iii)	• Exchange of information/exchanging/swapping information/information from being exchanged/information exchanges • In peace/at peace/alone	2
	(c)	(i)	• See/view/look at (your) available days/see what days are available/see the free/spare days • Manage/organise (your) time/timetable • Improve/make better/better the quality of work	3
		(ii)	(You will) feel <u>more</u> calm/peaceful/at peace/tranquil/calmer	1
2.	(a)	(i)	• BOX 2 NB If you tick 3 boxes = 1 mark • BOX 4 If you tick 4 boxes = 0 marks	2
		(ii)	• New/latest/recent/just out (films/movies/releases/productions) • (Films) from the 70s	2
	(b)	(i)	• Being outside/outdoors/in the open/fresh air makes you (get) hungry • Everyone <u>loves</u>/people <u>love</u> having a snack/snacking/nibbling/picking at food/bite to eat **(Any 1 from 2)**	1
		(ii)	• Homemade popcorn • Various/different/range of flavours of (milk)shakes • Refreshing drinks **(Any 2 from 3)**	2

Question			Expected Response(s)	Max mark
2.	(c)	(i)	The wardrobe(s)/clothes/costumes used in famous Spanish films/used clothes in famous Spanish films	1
		(ii)	• Silver jewellery • Wooden toys **(Any 1 from 2)**	1
	(d)		The relaxing sound/noise of the waves/sea/ocean/the sound of the relaxing waves	1
3.	(a)		• Air pollution/contamination/contaminated air • Destruction of forest(s)/wood<u>s</u>/woodland/deforestation	2
	(b)	(i)	• Change (our) habits • Have/adopt a <u>more</u> ecological/environmentally/eco-friendly (way of) life/lifestyle/style of life • Make/do a collective/joint/group effort/effort together **(Any 2 from 3)**	2
		(ii)	• Only buy/purchase what is necessary/what you/they need • Recycle as much as possible/as much as they can/as many things as possible **(Any 1 from 2)**	1
	(c)	(i)	• Take photos of environmental damage/harm/damaged environment • Make/do/paint a mural <u>in the club</u> • Inform/tell/explain to (their) families about (their) clean(-up) plan(s)/plans for cleaning **(Any 2 from 3)**	2
		(ii)	Small/little (work) groups	1
	(d)	(i)	Positive attitude(s) (about their role in society)	1
		(ii)	(The importance of) protecting/protection of the planet for future generations/the next generation	1

Writing

Please see the assessment criteria for Writing on pages 106–108.

Listening

Question			Expected response(s)	Max mark
1.	(a)		10 days	1
	(b)		The office was very far from her house	1
	(c)		• Answer/pick up the telephone/calls • Send e-mails • Make/prepare coffee	3
	(d)	(i)	• Very/really nice • She got on (very) well (with them/her colleagues) **(Any 1 from 2)**	1
		(ii)	Dined/had dinner	1
	(e)		Don't earn/get/make money/don't get paid	1
2.	(a)		• (Works) in a shoe shop • (Works) weekends/at the end of the week • Easy • Varied/Variable • Wouldn't like to do this type of work **(Any 2 from 5)**	2
	(b)		• In a team • Lots of responsibility • Work with nice/friendly/kind people/colleagues **(Any 2 from 3)**	2
	(c)		Abroad/in a foreign country	1
	(d)	(i)	• Journalism • Politics	2
		(ii)	• Good opportunity • <u>Has to/needs to/must</u> become/be independent • Meet/get to know new people **(Any 2 from 3)**	2
	(e)	(i)	Travel in/through/across/around Latin/South America	1
		(ii)	• Needs/requires lots of money • Has to save	2

Acknowledgements

Permission has been sought from all relevant copyright holders and Hodder Gibson is grateful for the use of the following:

Image © Alexander Gordeyev/Shutterstock.com (2016 Reading page 2);
Image © De Visu/Shutterstock.com (2016 Reading page 4);
Image © fonzales/Shutterstock.com (2016 Reading page 6);
Image © racorn/Shutterstock.com (2017 Reading page 2);
Image © gpointstudio/Shutterstock.com (2017 Reading page 4);
Image © Maksym Yemelyanov/stock.adobe.com (2017 Reading page 6);
Image © Corepics/stock.adobe.com (2018 Reading page 2);
Image © Vinicius Tupinamba/Shutterstock.com (2018 Reading page 4);
Image © Julio Aldana/Shutterstock.com (2018 Reading page 6).